VALLEY PARK
ELEMENTARY LIBRARY.

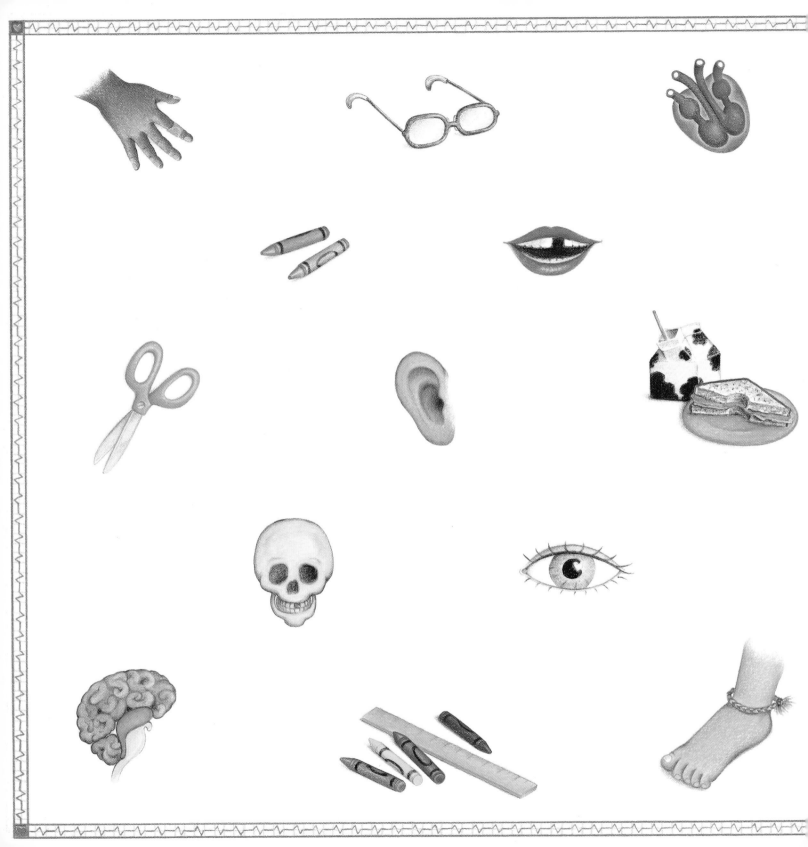

ME AND MY
AMAZING BODY

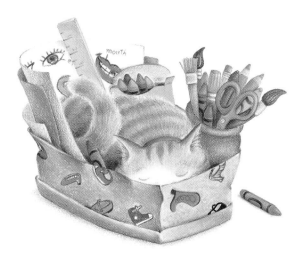

by Joan Sweeney   illustrated by Annette Cable

Dragonfly Books®   Crown Publishers • New York

Also by Joan Sweeney and Annette Cable

ME ON THE MAP

ME AND MY PLACE IN SPACE

ME AND MY FAMILY TREE

ME COUNTING TIME: FROM SECONDS TO CENTURIES

For my amazing son, John, the doctor —J.S.

To all children—take care of and be happy with your bodies.
This is your gift to yourself. —A.C.

DRAGONFLY BOOKS® PUBLISHED BY CROWN PUBLISHERS

Text copyright © 1999 by Joan Sweeney
Illustrations copyright © 1999 by Annette Cable

Published by Crown Publishers, a division of Random House, Inc., 1540 Broadway, New York, NY 10036

www.randomhouse.com/kids

Library of Congress Cataloging-in-Publication Data
Sweeney, Joan, 1930–
Me and my amazing body / by Joan Sweeney ; illustrated by Annette Cable.
p.   cm.
Summary: A girl describes how her skin, bones, muscles, brain, blood, heart, lungs,
and stomach receive energy and function as parts of her body.
1. Human anatomy—Juvenile literature. [1. Human anatomy. 2. Human physiology. 3. Body, Human.]
I. Cable, Annette, ill. II. Title.
QM27.S94   1999
[611]—dc21   98-34628

ISBN 0-517-80053-5 (trade)
0-517-80054-3 (lib. bdg.)
0-375-80623-7 (pbk.)

First Dragonfly Books® edition: May 2000

Printed in the United States of America
10 9 8 7 6 5

This is me and my amazing body.

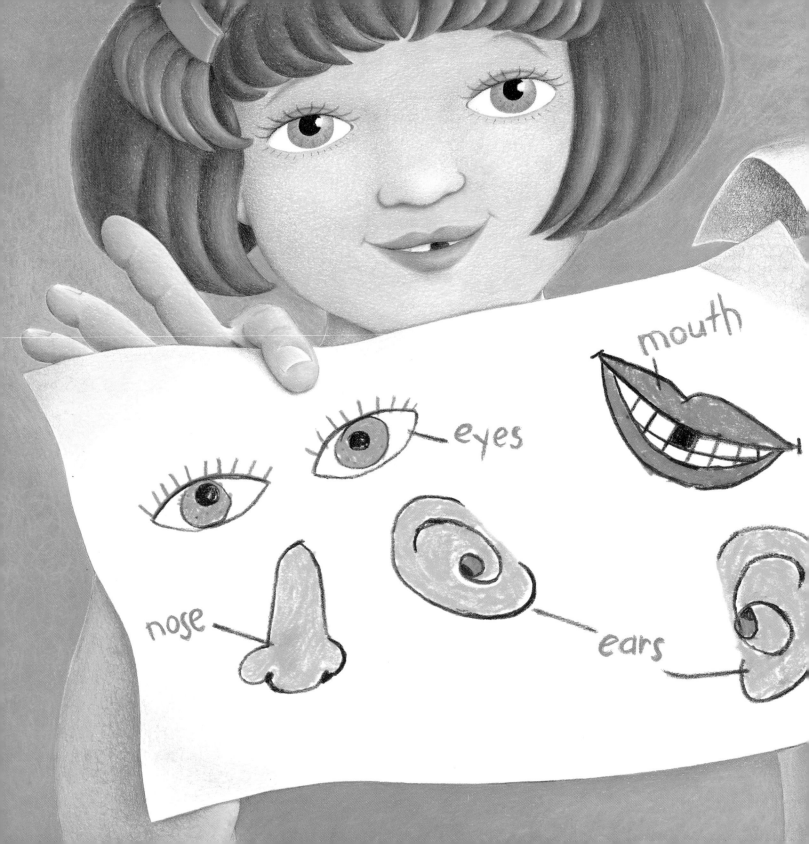

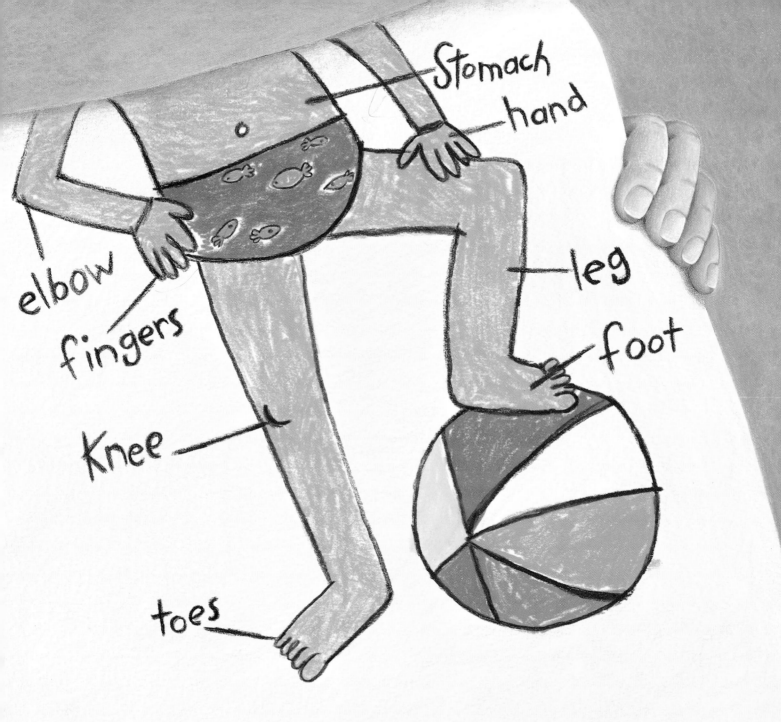

These are the parts of my body that I can see.

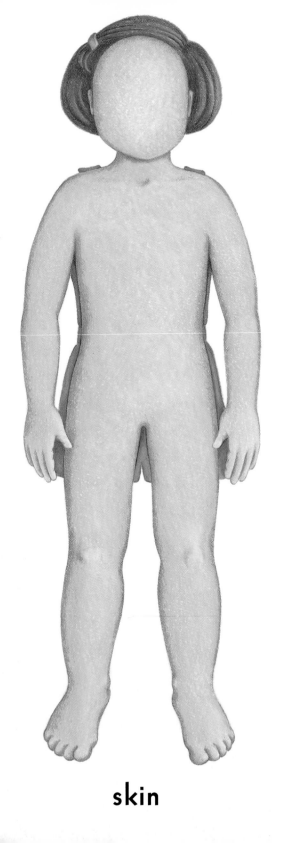

skin

But most of my body I *can't* see, because my **skin** covers almost every inch of it. Skin comes in many different colors. It holds my body together and lets me feel things, like my kitty's soft fur or the prickly spikes of my cactus. Ouch!

bones

Beneath my skin are my **bones**. All 206 of them! When my bones are put together, they're called a skeleton. My skeleton holds up my skin, just like tent poles hold up a tent. Bones are hard and help protect the softer insides of my body

My body and my brain need lots of energy to work well. They get energy from my **blood**. Blood contains oxygen from the air and nourishment from the food that I eat. My blood travels all over my body through special tubes called veins and arteries. If I cut or scrape my skin and it bleeds, don't worry! My body is always making more blood.

My blood can't move through my body all by itself. It needs my **heart**—a group of strong muscles in my chest—to move it. My heart is like my own little engine. It pumps blood through my body all the time, even when I'm sleeping! If I put my hand on my chest, I can feel my heart beating.

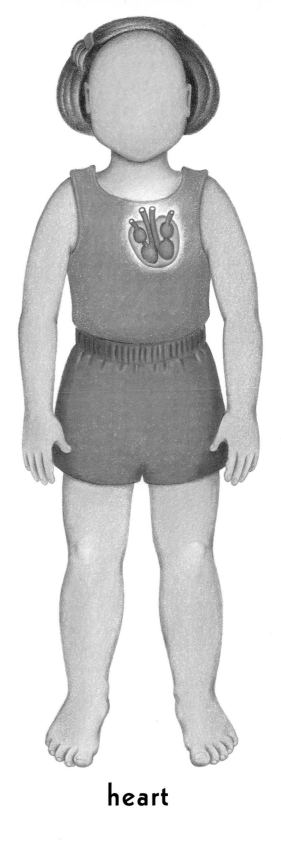

heart

I can also feel my **lungs** working when I breathe in deep. My lungs fill with fresh air like balloons and send the part of the air that I need—the oxygen—into my blood.

Then my lungs push the used air back out. A moment later, I breathe in fresh air all over again.

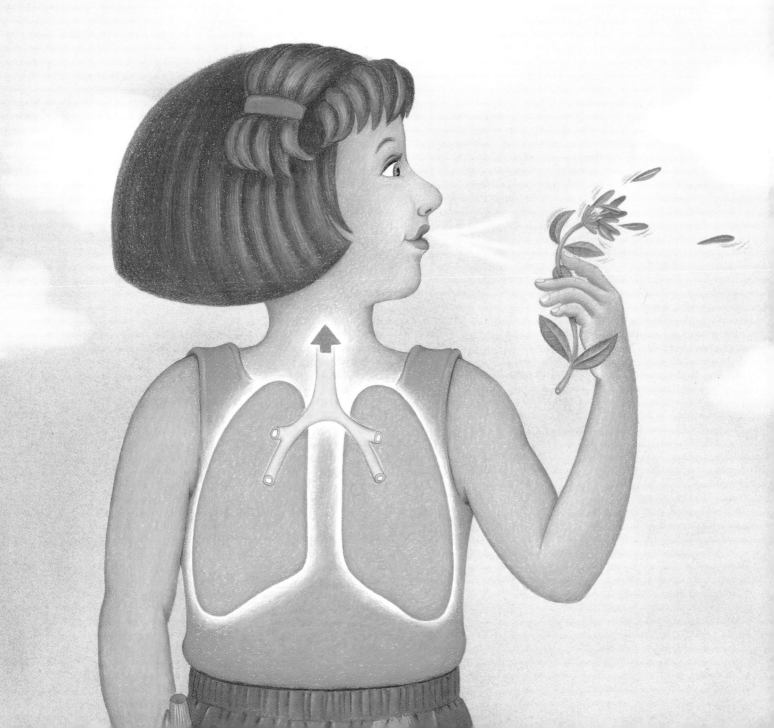

My body needs food along with air—or else I wouldn't grow! When I get hungry I eat, and the food goes down into my **stomach**. After I eat, my stomach mashes the food into very tiny pieces. Then my body takes what it needs for energy and growth, and gets rid of whatever it doesn't need.

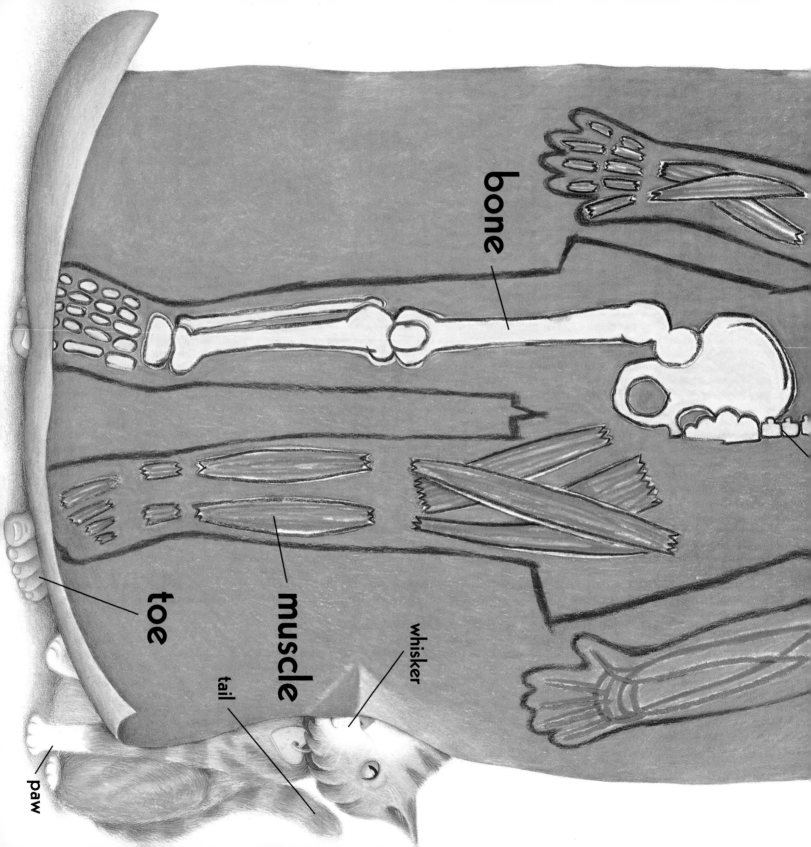

bone

toe

muscle

whisker

tail

paw

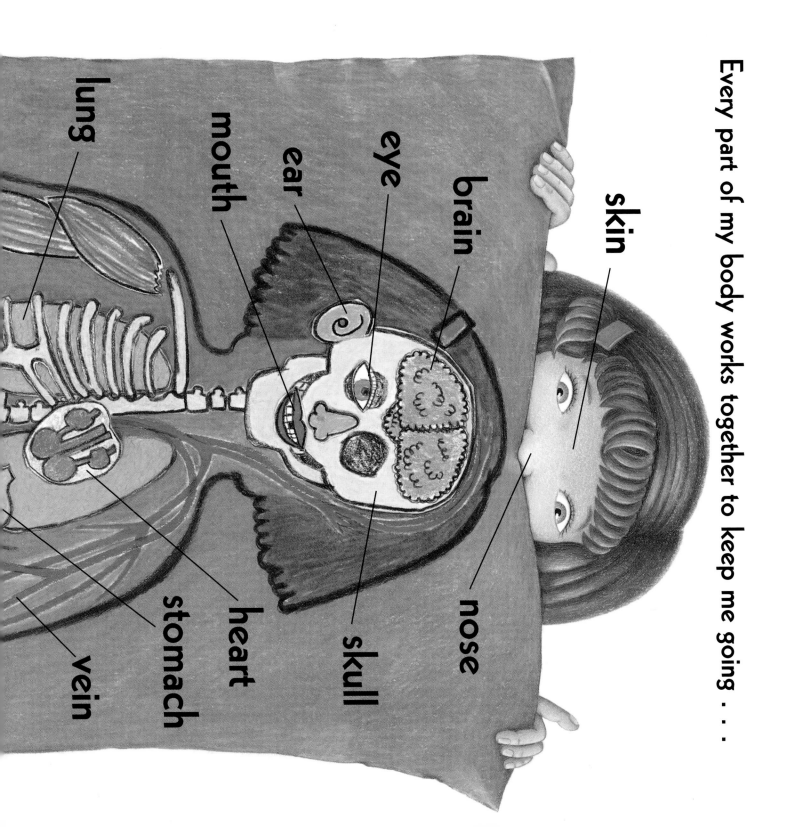

Every part of my body works together to keep me going . . .

skin

brain

eye

ear

mouth

lung

nose

skull

heart

stomach

vein

. . . and keep me growing.
And someday I'll be all
grown up!
   Isn't it amazing?

And most amazing of all—every person in the world has a body that's very much the same, but every person is also very different.

There's no one else in the world exactly like you. And no one exactly like me.

Or ever will be!

AMAZING BODY FACTS

Your stomach digests about 2,190 quarts of food each year. That's around 8,760 bowls of spaghetti!

Over half of your body's bones are in your hands and feet. That's more than 100 bones!

If you could line up all your blood vessels, they would wrap around the world *four* times!

When you sneeze, air comes out of your lungs at over 100 miles per hour!

Your brain weighs only about three pounds, but it can store billions of bits of information.

The heart beats around three billion times in an average person's life.

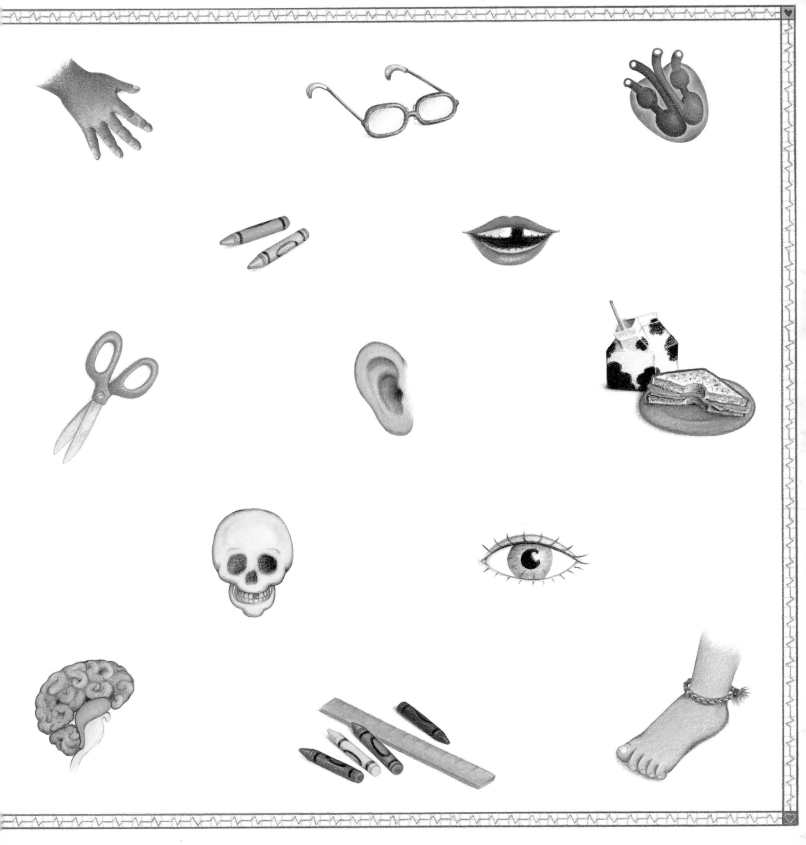